Re-Quoted

Between what's told and what's felt

Naina Das

BookLeaf Publishing

India | USA | UK

Made with ❤ on the BookLeaf Publishing Platform
www.bookleafpub.in
www.bookleafpub.com

Dedication

Love you Mom and Dad,

For every pen I've held so tight
You were the ink that helped me write
Your love and care, so true and strong,
have been with me all along.
This heart, this quiet art
has always been your loving part.

Preface

We often read quotes and hold onto them like truths. But what about the side we never hear? The feelings left behind, the questions unasked?

This book is a collection of thoughts, ones that kept me awake at night or surfaced while sipping my coffee, wondering about the things we're told but never fully explained. The other side of the story is the part no one talks about. Each poem in this collection is a conversation with a quote and sometimes a challenge to it. Your teen years teach you a lot. As you grow, your lens changes. You start understanding yourself differently and life begins to reveal new layers. In between all that change, you find words. This book is made of those words.

I hope these verses reach both sides of you; the one that finds comfort in the familiar as well as the one that dares to feel differently.

Acknowledgements

To my family, each of you has helped me see the best in me. You've taught me to write with my heart and never fear where it leads. To my friends, thank you for reading my early lines and telling me they made you feel something real and think with depth. Your words made me believe it was worth sharing. To my teachers, thank you for helping me grow not just as a writer but as a thinker beyond the page.

To the beautiful strangers who stumble upon my writings, your quiet reading means more than you know. You remind me that words can travel and still feel close. If even one of these poems speaks to you then I know this book has done what it came here to do.

To myself, thank you for holding on. For writing through the silence and the days it felt like no one was listening. You turned thoughts into poems, and poems into something worth sharing.

Thank you for reading between the lines!

1. Time heals everything

Time
Just a clicking clock
Its hands moving endlessly forward
Minutes pass, hours fade and it never stops
You sit there wondering
Do they ever pause? Just for a moment?

Whether things are right or wrong, good or bad
The moment still slips away
Everything around you seems to change
And yet
The pain within you remains the same
They told you,
"Time heals."
So you listened.
You gave it space
A day
A month
A year.

But nothing changed.
You're still here
Standing in the same place
Carrying the same ache
Maybe it's no longer visible,
But you know how deeply it hides inside you.

Time heals, right?
You followed every step
just like they said
So why are you still stuck?
Why does it still feel like you're in the beginning?
The truth is
healing is terrifying
Because no one ever taught us how to do it.

Time only keeps moving
Constant, quiet, uncaring.
But healing
Healing isn't in time itself
It's in you.

It's in the moments when you wake up
Tired and worn down
Yet still choose to show up for yourself
It's in the days when the weight feels too heavy
But you sit with it anyway

And let it sting
Because sometimes, that's all you can do.
You feel it
All of it.

And somewhere in that stillness
In those long, aching pauses
You begin to realize
Healing isn't what time does to you.
It's what you choose to do with your time.

2. The grass is greener on the other side

Why is it that we always find ourselves pulled under
By the weight of what others have done?
That sharp-edged word
"comparison"
Cuts into us so easily
Making us question who we are
Even when we haven't paused to really look in the
mirror.

I glance out the window
A pretty tree, full and free.
"Damn, that looks better than mine"
I whisper,
"I wish I had that too."
Some marks I missed,
And thought
Maybe then I'd be proud if some more.
A newer phone in hand,
Still I don't feel any fuller.

Because the grass
So silky and clean
Shimmers brighter across the line.
But I never told you
About the days
I didn't bother watering my own.

Wait, could it be me
Overlooking myself?
So I paused.
Gave it thought.
Gave it effort.
Poured some love into my yard.

And slowly,
It grew.
Not perfect.
But real.
Alive and mine.

It's far too easy to look over the fence
And assume someone else's life is effortless
Like their path was laid out better than ours.
But the only thing I have ever truly been able to control
Is how I choose to feel about my own life.

So now
Instead of chasing what others have
I only compare myself
To who I was yesterday.
That's the only green
I ever want to grow.

3. Be yourself

All I hear is them saying
"Be yourself. Be true."
But who am I?
And who are you
To tell me that
When every time I show up real
The world sees it as a flaw?
"Too kind."
"Too soft."
"Too much."

That was me being me.
So slowly
We put on masks.
We shape-shift.
We dim.
We shrink.
Until one day
We don't even recognize the reflection anymore.

And I wonder
Am I betraying them
Or betraying myself?
But here's the truth,
Be yourself even then.
Even when it's hard.
Even when they don't get it.
Even when they leave.

Because the ones who matter
Will see you.
Really see you.
And stay.
It's not worth hiding so deeply
That you lose the connection with your own soul.

Be yourself.
Not to fit in.
Not to please.
Not to be liked.

Be yourself
Because it brings you peace.
Because it makes you happy.
Because you deserve a life where you can breathe,
Unmasked. Unfiltered. Free.
So give the real you a chance to exist.

4. Forgive and forget

"Move on."
Two words made to sound so simple.
But it's not.
People hurt.
And sometimes
The hurt lingers
Far longer than the closeness ever did.

But think of it this way
Even if things ended,
I'll still remember the good.
The laughs.
The moments that once made me smile.

And forgiveness?
It's never really about them.
It's about me.
It's about accepting
That I had no idea things would turn out this way.

A friendship broken.
A relationship lost.
A fight with a neighbor.
The pet that never made it their age.
The day your mind turned against you.
The time you said too much or too little.
It's okay to feel it all.
Don't push it down,
Don't pretend it's gone.
Because forgetting doesn't work
Until you face what you're trying to forget.

So I chose forgiveness.
Not because they asked.
But because I needed peace for them and so for me.

Why wish bad
When we're all just humans,
Struggling quietly
Trying to survive?
A little kindness even in your thoughts
Can be healing.

"Forget", that word never really made sense to me.
You can't erase pain.
You can't undo memory.
But you can choose how it shapes you.

So don't forget what happened.
Learn from it. Grow with it.

And most importantly,
Forgive yourself.
For trusting.
For hoping.
For loving.
For breaking.
For trying.
You didn't fail.
You simply lived.

5. Everything happens for a reason

"Everything happens for a reason"
that's what we're told.
So our minds begin to race
Piecing together thoughts like broken glass
Searching for something, anything at all
That could explain the ache.

We try to find meaning
In moments that shattered us
Because maybe, just maybe
If we knew why, it would hurt a little less.
But what about the times when there is no reason?
No lesson tucked behind the pain,
No greater plan written in the stars.
Just silence.
Just ache.

And sometimes
The reason isn't even ours to carry.

It was someone else's choice,
Someone else's mistake,
But here we are
Left to heal
From wounds we never signed up for.
That's the cycle, isn't it?
Their actions.
Our consequences.
Their chaos.
Our healing.

So we start asking
Can I even trust people again?
Can I trust myself again?
The truth is, the moment you start trusting yourself
Really, deeply trusting your heart to carry you
You stop needing the comfort of every "why."
You stop clinging to explanations
And start leaning into your own strength.

Situations will happen.
They won't always make sense.
And no quote or phrase
Will ever fully wrap around the ache.
But when you don't find a reason,
Let the reason be you.

Let it be your choice to grow,
To soften without breaking,
To keep going without answers.
Go in with hope,
Come out with strength.
That's more than any reason,
And its enough.

6. Communication is the key

"Communication"
It's meant to be the bridge between two
The way we speak our truth
So someone else might hear us
Without questioning why we feel the way we do.

We humans carry different minds,
Different pasts and different hearts.
Yet somehow, we find it so hard to compromise
Because how many times can you keep giving in?
What's the balance between understanding and losing
yourself?

Communication is a step
But comprehension?
That's just as important.
What happens when you're good with words
When you try your best to explain
But the other person still won't understand you?
What do you do then?

Do you leave it?
Let it sit heavy in your chest
And carry on like it doesn't matter?

I understand.
I always do.
It's almost instinct now
To read between the lines
To comfort before being comforted
To make room for others even when there's no room left
for me.
But sometimes
Just once
I wish someone understood me
The way I try so hard to understand them.

There are days when you'll speak and speak
And the other person will hear your words
But not really listen.
Because our minds are always racing
So quick to reply,
So eager to defend,
That we forget to sit still in someone else's silence.
And without empathy,
What is communication really worth?

But still, I hold on to the hope

That one day, we'll learn to speak softer
To listen deeper,
To pause before reacting,
To choose clarity over assumptions,
And love over ego.

Because real connection
Only asks for honesty,
A little patience,
And a heart willing to hear,
Even when it hurts.

And maybe then
We'll finally see that communication isn't just about
talking
It's about understanding.
And that kind of understanding
Can heal almost anything.

7. Do good and good comes back

"Do good, and good comes back"
For the longest time
I believed it with everything I had.
Because I know the way I am
I know how deeply I care
How freely I give
Maybe sometimes too much.
But that's just the way I've always been.

In a world that can be too cruel
Too rushed, too cold,
I never wanted to follow its rhythm.
I wanted to be the quiet good
In a crowd that had forgotten softness.
Not for reward.
Not for praise.
Just because, I believed in being the change
Even when it felt lonely.
But somewhere along the way

This saying started to hurt.
Because I waited.
Waited for the good to come back.
For the appreciation.
For the kind of love I gave so easily.

Well life taught me a hard truth
That no matter how kind you are,
Not everyone will notice
Not everyone will thank you
And not everyone will stay
But maybe that's okay.

Because real kindness
Was never meant to be a transaction
Still, I'd be lying
If I said I never sat in silence,
Hoping it would come back from the same people
I once gave everything to.

But the good?
It came.
Not from them.
But from others
In unexpected places.
I found it in animals
Eyes that held no judgment,

Only presence.
Love, pure and gentle
The kind I spent so long chasing
Was right there in front of me
I just hadn't been looking.
Because I was too stuck on
Wanting it from the ones
Who never knew how to give it back.

So yes do good
Not because it'll return the same way
Not because someone owes you
But because somewhere
In this world,
That good will circle back to you.
Not always from the same hands
But from the right ones.

8. Be the change you want to see in others

Be the change you wish to see in the world
As simple as it sounds
There's a quiet kind of power in it.
There's beauty in learning
From your own mistakes
And even more in the ones made by others.
Because in those reflections
You begin to understand the kind of person you needed.

When you were at your lowest
When everything felt too heavy to carry.
So instead of waiting for someone to show up
You become that someone.
Be the friend you once longed for.
Be the family you wished would understand you.
Be the love you spent years looking for.

But here's what nobody tells you
When you change, you begin to hope others will too.

You expect your effort to echo,
Your healing to inspire,
Your softness to soften them.
You think and think
"If I can shift, maybe they'll meet me halfway."

But expectations are fragile things.
They grow silently and break loudly.
Because people don't always change
Just because you did.
You sit with that frustration
And it hurts.

Because you weren't just changing for yourself
You were hoping your growth would bring them closer.
And when it doesn't,
It feels like a personal failure.

Change isn't always mirrored
Sometimes, it's just witnessed.
You grow,
And they may never follow.

You realize
Changing isn't about fixing others
It's about freeing yourself
From cycles you no longer wish to repeat.

From versions of you that no longer feel like home.

And in that,
You become the change
It starts something.
Not always in those you hoped
But always in those who are ready.

9. Honesty is the best policy

"Honesty is the best policy"
Sure it sounds noble
Like the right thing to do.
And often it is.

I failed a test once
The kind that makes your stomach drop
And your heart beat a little faster
When you think of telling your parents.
But I did.
And I told my mom,
"At least I didn't cheat like the rest."
And a part of me felt proud
Because I knew what I stood for
Even if the grade didn't show it

Just honesty.
We make mistakes.
Things go wrong.
But I never pretended otherwise.

Still, I couldn't help but wonder
What do you really get from being honest?

Because sometimes
Truth doesn't earn you praise.
It earns you consequences.
It earns you disappointment from others,
Even when you're already carrying your own.

I know I'm truthful.
I know I stand by what I do.
But honesty doesn't always feel like the reward they
promised.
And yet,
Lying doesn't sit well either
So where's the balance?

I've learned this
It's not always about speaking every truth
But knowing how and when to speak it
It's about honesty that holds kindness
Not just bluntness.
It's about reading the room
And choosing words that don't just speak the truth
But also carry care.

Because yes

Sometimes honesty hurts.
Sometimes silence has value.
And sometimes,
The most honest thing you can do
Is pause
Breathe
And ask yourself
Is this truth necessary now?
Is it kind?
Is it mine to tell?

That's the honesty they don't teach in school
The kind that's not just about facts
But about feelings.
Not just about being right
But being real.
With yourself.
With others.
And with the world.

10. A problem shared is a problem halved

There have been times
When speaking out made me feel lighter
Like maybe the world wasn't closing in on me
But then there were the other times
The ones where people listened
only to reply
or worse, to judge.
Where what I shared
became a reason for labels,
called an attention seeker,
or just too much.

And it hurt
Because you wonder
if expressing yourself is meant to help
why does it sometimes leave deeper bruises?

It makes you afraid
Afraid to speak

Afraid to suppress
Because both feel like losing.

So what next?
How do you find the comfort
In sharing what storms inside you
Without the fear of being misunderstood?
Truth is, there's no one answer

Some days
I try
Over and over
Testing ways that fit me, not the world.
And in that search, I found writing
Not for likes.
Not for applause.
Not even for someone else to read.
But for me.

To feel heard by my own heart
To see my emotions written out,
naked and real.
It taught me that sometimes
you aren't waiting for people to understand.
You're waiting for yourself to listen.

Speaking doesn't always have a perfect way.

There will be stumbles.
Wrong people.
Wrong moments.

But keep trying
There will be a few quiet, kind who hold space
without needing to fix you.
And in those rare places
A problem shared
will feel a little lighter.

11. Slow and steady wins the race

But does it always?
Sometimes life isn't really a race
Or it's one you didn't even sign up for

No one tells us that sometimes opportunities don't wait
for slow
They don't always reward steady
They look for unprepared but brave
For the ones who jump before overthinking.
Who mess up.
Who learn midair
Being too careful can lock you out of chances.

There's a difference between being patient and being
passive.
It's like traffic
we're all trying to reach somewhere
rushing, honking, stuck at signals, irritated.
And yet no one pauses to ask

Why am I rushing? Or where am I even going?
The truth is
the race isn't about speed.
It's about timing.
Knowing when to slow down
When to risk it all
When to hit pause and let yourself heal.

Competitive exams, career milestones, social validations
it's easy to start running because others are.
But there was this one saying that stuck with me
"If you're in a rat race and you win, you're still a rat."
Winning isn't the point.

The point is what you've learnt about yourself
while running, walking, pausing or even falling.
Patience isn't about waiting your turn to win the race
It's about understanding yourself in the process.
Knowing when that 'break' you needed turns into self-
sabotage
and pulling yourself back up with everything you've got.

And maybe life isn't about reaching the finish line first.
It's about running your own race, on your own terms

12. In unity there is strength

A group of some can make things happen.
You follow, you believe
like no one else ever could
That's what I always carried

A group of friends should feel like strength, right?
A safe place to deal with any and everything.
But unity isn't always what it's made out to be
It's not the kind I believed in for so long

Sometimes, we bond over negativity
Over the gossip, the complaining, the quick judgments of
others
Rarely stopping to look at ourselves in the mirror
Ever notice how in a crowd,
people stop thinking for themselves?
How easy it is to get pulled into
a wave of opinions that aren't even yours?

Unity should never mean losing your voice in the noise.

It should be a space
to share, to speak, to be.
To stick together but not feel invisible within it.

Friendships take steps forward, you bond so well
You laugh, you understand, you trust.
But over time you'll learn to ask yourself
Did I lose myself here?
Or did I find myself within this so called strength of
unity?

Sometimes, we get so blinded by belonging
We forget to have opinions of our own.
And you know what?
That's okay
Because noticing it is the first step
To rebuilding a unity where you're not afraid to be you.

13. Hardwork matters

Hard work pays off
I'm sure it does
You put so much into something
just to feel it at the end
Cook for hours and there it is the taste of your effort
Study for days and those marks feel like
little victories you earned alone
Hit the gym for months and that firm pump
reminds you you're not the same as before
Journal for a while and slowly
your mood, your mind, your heart
they shift.

It's what I take from every single day
To work so hard. To never give up.
But no one really tells you about the exhaustion you'll
drag along with it
About the way you'll keep working, chasing, striving
Yet feel this weird sense of more
Like you should be doing even more.

I'm doing hard work, right?
So what's the problem now?

The thing is
I work so much that I forget to breathe
I barely sleep. Coffee runs through my veins.
And for the longest time, I told myself it's peaceful,
right?
Escaping the noise of the world in something positive.
Productivity made me feel safe.
But damn, I was tired.

I didn't need to quit.
But I did need to pause.
To realize that sometimes, taking a break is also hard
work.
To rest your mind
To feel proud for the things you already did
Because hard work pays off
But only when you let it pay off before it drains you dry

Let your efforts breathe.
Let yourself breathe.
That's part of the work too.
And it'll be as much hard

14. Sharing something means seeking for advice

If someone is sharing something they seeking for advice
That's what people believe, don't they?
The moment you open up about what's weighing you
down
There's always this flood of suggestions
Do this.
Leave that.
Move on.
Don't think too much.
And yes sometimes those words land right
Sometimes they help

But most times?
I wasn't looking to be fixed.
I wasn't waiting for advice.
I was waiting to be heard.
To feel like what I'm carrying matters
without someone labeling it or rushing to solve it

Because there's a kind of peace
in someone just sitting with you in your mess.
No advice.
No judgment.
No 'you should.'
Just a 'I hear you.'

And it's true what they say
Most advice is people talking to their past selves
Trying to save someone else from what they once
drowned in
It's human, I get it.

But maybe next time you hear someone vent,
don't be so quick to fix it
Ask yourself:
Are you speaking for them or are you comforting your
old self through them?

Because trust me
Some days all a person wants
is a safe place to fall apart
No advice.
No lesson.
Just space.

And sometimes that's more than what's needed

15. Sorry brings change

Sorry brings change
That's what people say
I've always heard that if you're really sorry about
something,
you'd change.
Not because someone asked you to
Not because you got caught
But because it bothered you
Because it stayed in your head,
made you uncomfortable,
made you question yourself a little.

But I don't think most of us are taught what to do after a
sorry
We think saying it fixes everything
As if that word of just five letters thrown into the air
can vanish what happened
But it doesn't.

It's easy to say sorry

Way too easy actually.
I've said it for things I didn't even feel bad about
sometimes
just to keep the peace, just to make it stop, just because
it felt expected.
And people have said it to me too
And then do the exact same thing the next day.
It's exhausting, isn't it?

Because sorry was never supposed to be the end
It's supposed to be the beginning
Of a conversation.
Of a change.
Of you learning about yourself and how you make other
people feel.
Its important to me, what about you?

And the tough part is
sometimes you realize that
you don't actually want to change
You're just sorry they felt bad.
You're just sorry it became a thing.
But deep down you know
you're gonna do it again because it's easier
than fixing yourself.

I've been there too

I've hurt people without meaning to
I've apologized like it was nothing.
I've forgiven people because they said sorry
but felt stupid about it later when it happened again
Over time I started to watch actions more than words.

Because a real sorry isn't what you say,
it's what you show.
And it's not instant either.
Change takes time.
It takes messing up, catching yourself, feeling that guilt
settle in your stomach
Then making the decision to be better
not because someone's watching,
Cause you don't like the version of yourself
that keeps repeating that mistake

Sorry does brings change
But only if you let it.
Only if you mean it.
Only if you don't treat it like a shield to hide behind.

And maybe, it's okay to not be perfect at it
As long as you're honest about it
Just cause sorry without change is just a word.
And words mean nothing
if they don't feel heavy when you say them

16. Maturity comes as you grow older

Maturity comes as you grow older
That's what they say when you're younger
You look at adults and think it's cool
No rules, no limits
You make your own moves
They tell you that once you're mature, you'll get it

But turning 18 doesn't mean you're ready to live them
Being an adult isn't about a number or age
It's about what you learn at every stage
It comes from the days you fall down so hard
And still find a way to move forward
From mistakes you made and lessons you keep
From nights you cried yourself to sleep

Maturity isn't about acting tough
Or pretending you've had enough
It's knowing when to stay
When to leave

When to hold on and
when to breathe.

It's being kind, even when you're hurt
Choosing peace over proving your worth
It's taking what life throws at you
And finding something good to hold on to
It's not about age, money or pride
It's about keeping a little light inside

Growing, healing and being true
Not just for others,
but for you too.
So no
Maturity doesn't show up one day
It's built slowly along the way
You'll know you've grown, not when they say you do
But when you look at yourself, and feel proud too!

17. Trust the process

People often told me to simply trust the process
When life got tough
When I had no clue where I was going
So I did,
I trusted the process

But what we take from that quote
is to believe it'll happen on its own
no chasing, no questioning
Just wait is what they say
It'll all work out they said again

And that word TRUST
Over time slowly chipped away at me
Because when you've been let down enough times
You start putting your faith in everything but yourself
You trust the timing, the universe, the process
everything except your own hands and your own heart.

So when nothing changes right away

you start thinking maybe it's you who's broken
Maybe you were never meant to get there
Broken trust convinces you
that hope will fix it all for you
That if you just wait long enough
the right people, the right path, the right life will
somehow fall into place.

But the thing is
hope needs you just as much as you need it.
You can't trust the process if you're standing still and
hiding from your own life.
You can't trust the future if you don't show up for the
present.
Trusting the process doesn't mean disappearing.
It doesn't mean letting life drag you somewhere without
your say.
It doesn't mean waiting for someone else to rescue you.

It means trusting yourself to be part of the process.
It means believing that every tiny decision you make
Even the messy ones is building something.
It means standing back up after the trust you gave away
shattered,
and trusting again
But this time, trusting yourself first.

Because the process isn't some magic happening far
away

You are the process.
You always were.

18. You can be kind and still say no

Kindness has always been a part of me
Something I carried everywhere I went
Something I wove into conversations and quiet spaces
Something I gave even when no one asked for it
because that is just how my heart worked
I loved being kind

Seeing the way it softened a room
The way it turned heavy days into lighter ones
It made me believe I was doing something good,
meaningful and real
But somewhere along the way
I forgot to be kind to myself
I stayed longer in places that drained me
I agreed when my heart screamed no
I gave and gave until I had nothing left inside me
and even then I wondered if I was doing enough

Being kind became a habit, a duty, a silent expectation

I forgot that kindness was supposed to be a choice,
not a sacrifice
One day I realized
kindness without boundaries is not kindness at all
It is an apology for existing
It is telling yourself you do not deserve the same care
the one you offer to everyone else

So I started learning something new
I started saying no when my body felt tired
I started leaving when my soul felt empty
I started protecting my peace as fiercely as I protected
others

And here is what no one tells you
When you begin to choose yourself
Not all will understand
They will call you rude
They will call you selfish
They will question the goodness they once praised

But selfish was never meant to be an insult
Selfish simply means you are giving yourself
the same love you spent years giving away
You can be kind and still say no
You can love others and still choose yourself

You can offer softness without breaking your own heart
to pieces

It will feel strange at first
It will hurt in ways you cannot explain
but one day you will realize
you were never meant to set yourself on fire
just to keep others warm

Kindness was never meant to cost you your own soul
Kindness was meant to be a bridge and never a burden
And the greatest kindness you will ever offer
is the one you finally offer yourself

19. Closure comes when the story ends

Closure is something that feels necessary
when something unexpected happens
when you are left searching for a reason
searching for something to hold on to
to believe it is really over
to believe there is nothing more left to say

It feels like a final page you are desperate to turn,
understand
and finally accept it
To move forward without wondering
what could have been

But here is the other side
the one no one prepares you for
The times when you wait for closure and..
it never arrives
The times when you sit in the middle of the silence
hearing nothing but your own heart

trying to make sense of the wreckage left behind
There is a door behind you
still slightly open
still whispering the answers you will never hear

And what then?
Where does closure come from?
when the other person leaves without a word,
when distance builds without confrontation,
when confusion is met with more confusion,
when no one dares to ask what went wrong??
Because pretending it never mattered feels easier than
admitting it did.

What then?
Where do you find your ending is left half-told, half-
loved
Sometimes the hardest truth is this
Closure does not always come wrapped in explanations,
or apologies
Not even conversations
Sometimes closure is not something you receive
It is something you decide
It is something you build with your own hands
out of the ruins left behind

Because silence too

is an answer
That you deserve to move forward
even if the story never got the ending you wished for
You deserve to close the door
even if no one else stands there to say goodbye

Closure comes when you accept
that not all stories are meant to be complete
Closure comes when you realize
you are allowed to keep living
even if you never understand why they stopped being a
part of your life
Closure comes when you no longer wait
for someone else to hand it to you

Closure comes when you end the story for yourself

20. Healing isn't a straight line

Healing has its ups and downs.
Its bumps and then some bruises
I believed that
I understood that.

But no one talks about what it feels like
when you try so hard to heal
when you push yourself past the breaking points
when you exceed your own expectations
and you still fall
When after months of work
after moments where you thought you were finally free
you crash again
into the same feelings you thought you had buried long
ago.

It breaks your heart
It makes you question if
all the progress even meant anything at all

If anything you built within yourself
was ever strong enough to begin with

That is the part no one really prepares you for
The grief of having to meet yourself again
at the same pain you fought so hard to leave behind

But here is what I am learning
even if it is the hardest thing to believe right now
Falling does not mean you are starting over
It does not erase the miles you have already walked
It does not undo the days you chose to stay alive
when it would have been easier not to

It does not mean your healing was a lie
Progress is not measured by how far you get without
falling
It is measured by how many times you are willing to
stand up again.
Even when it feels unfair.
Even when it feels like you are fighting a battle
you should have already won

Healing is messy
It asks you to love yourself even when you feel
unlovable
It asks you to stay patient even when you are exhausted

It asks you to forgive yourself for still hurting
for still needing time
for still being human.

You are not broken because you fell
You are brave because you are willing to try again
Healing is not a destination you reach and stay
It is a journey you walk every single day

And today
even if you are hurting
even if you are tired
you are still healing.

21. The bravest thing you ever do is simply keep living

They say it like it is easy
like breathing and waking up is just part of the day
But sometimes living is the hardest thing you will ever
do

It is waking up with a heart that feels too heavy
It is carrying memories that ache in the quiet parts of
you
It is smiling when you want to cry
It is staying when you want to give up

The world was meant to be softer than this
People were meant to hold each other through the
storms
But somewhere we forgot
We started building walls around our hearts
and calling it strength
We learned to stay silent when we needed to speak
We learned to walk away before anyone else could

We learned to hide the parts of us that still longed for
connection
because it felt safer that way

Living is not about pretending to be unbreakable
It is about knowing you are breakable and still choosing
to stay
Choosing to breathe even when everything inside you
says it is too much

There is so much pain in this world
but there is also light
There are still hands that reach out
There are still words that heal
There are still mornings that feel like new chances
And maybe that is enough
Maybe that is everything

You are not just surviving
You are leaving traces of strength and hope behind
in ways you may never fully know
And maybe that is what bravery truly is
Choosing to live
even when it would be easier not to